SWU-NAP- 024

UNIFORMS OF RUSSIAN ARMY DURING THE NAPOLEONIC WAR VOL.19

UNDER THE REIGN OF ALEXANDER I
EMPEROR OF RUSSIA BETWEEN 1801 AND 1825
GUARDS GARRISON, INVALIDS AND MARINE ÉQUIPAGE

From the Viskovatov's greatest work:
"Historical description of the clothing and
arms of the Russian Army"

English translation by Mark Conrad

SOLDIERSHOP PUBLISHING

AUTHOR

Aleksandr Vasilevich Viskovatov born 22 April (4 May New Style) 1804, died 27 February (11 March) 1858 in St. Petersburg, Russian military historian. He graduated from the 1st Cadet Corps and served in the artillery, the hydrographic depot of the Naval Ministry, and then in the Department of Military Educational Institutions. He mainly studied historical artifacts and the histories of military units. Viskovatov's greatest work was the Historical Description of the Clothing and Arms of the Russian Army.

PUBLISHING'S NOTE

None of **unpublished** images or text of our book may be reproduced in any format without the expressed written permission of Soldiershop.com when not indicate as marked with license creative commons 3.0 or 4.0. The publisher remains to disposition of the possible having right for all the doubtful sources images or not identifies. Our trademark: Soldiershop Publishing ©, The names of our series: Soldiers&Weapons, Battlefield, War in colour, PaperSoldiers, Soldiershop e-book etc. are herein © by Soldiershop.com.

NOTE ABOUT BOOK PRINTING BEFORE 1925

This book may contain text or images coming from a reproduction of a book published before 1925 (over seventy years ago). No effort has been made to modernize or standardize the spelling used in the original text, so this book may have occasional imperfections such as missing or blurred pages, poor pictures, errant marks, etc. that were either part of the original artifact, or were introduced by the scanning process. We believe this work is culturally important, and despite the imperfections, have elected to bring it back into print (digital and/or paper) as part of our continuing commitment to the preservation of printed works worldwide. We appreciate your understanding of the imperfections in the preservation process, and hope you enjoy this valuable book. Now this book is purpose re-built and is proof-read and re-type set from the original to provide an outstanding experience of reflowing text, also for an ebook reader. However Soldiershop publishing added, enriched, revised and overhauled the text, images, etc. of the cover and the book. Therefore, the job is now to all intents and purposes a derivative work, and the added, new and original parts of the book are the copyright of Soldiershop. On this second unpublished part of the book none of images or text may be reproduced in any format without the expressed written permission of Soldiershop. Almost many of the images of our books and prints are taken from original first edition prints or books that are no longer in copyright and are therefore public domain. We have been a specialized bookstore for a long time so we (and several friends antiquarian booksellers) have readily available a lot of ancient, historical and illustrated books not in copyright. Each of our prints, art designs or illustrations is either our own creation, or a fully digitally restoration by our computer artists, or non copyrighted images. All of our prints are "tagged" with a registered digital copyright. Soldiershop remains to disposition of the possible having right for all the doubtful sources images or not identifies.

LICENSES COMMONS

Much of the text in this book are from the *"Memoirs of the Empress Catherine II., by Catherine II, Empress of Russia"* This book is for the use of anyone anywhere at no cost and with almost no restrictions whatsoever. You may copy it, give it away or re-use it under the terms of the similar creative commons License. This book may utilize material marked with license creative commons 3.0 or 4.0 (CC BY 4.0), (CC BY-ND 4.0), (CC BY-SA 4.0) or (CC0 1.0). We give appropriate attribution credit and indicate if change were made below in the acknowledgements field.

ACKNOWLEDGEMENTS

A Special Thanks to NYPL and other institutions for their kindly permission to use some images of his archives, collections or books used in our book.

Title: **UNIFORMS OF RUSSIAN ARMY DURING THE NAPOLEONIC WAR VOL. 19**
Guards Garrison, Invalids, marine équipage & Instructional corps By A.V.Viskovatov. Serie edit by Luca S. Cristini. First edition by Soldiershop. May 2018 Cover & Art Design: Luca S. Cristini. Plates re-colorations by Anna Cristini.
ISBN code: 978-88-93273473

Published by Soldiershop publishing, via Padre Davide, 7 - 24050 Zanica (BG) ITALY. wwwsoldiershop.com

UNIFORMS OF THE RUSSIAN ARMY DURING THE NAPOLEONIC WAR VOL. 19

UNDER THE REIGN OF ALEXANDER I EMPEROR OF
RUSSIA BETWEEN 1801 AND 1825
*
GUARDS GARRISON, INVALIDS, MARINE ÉQUIPAGE
& INSTRUCTIONAL CORPS

Tambour und Gemeiner der Kaiserl: Rußischen Artillerie.

Wien bey Johann Cappi.

▲ *Drummer and artillery man of Russian Imperial Artillery*

HISTORICAL DESCRIPTION OF THE CLOTHING AND ARMS OF THE RUSSIAN ARMY - A.V. VISKOVATOV
(First English translation by Mark Conrad)

Soldiershop is glad to presents the complete collection of the great job made by A.V. Viskovatov dedicated to the uniforms and weapons belonging to the Russian army during the Napoleonic period, until 1825. The time we considered corresponds to the reigns of two Tzars: Paul I, who reigned since 1769 until his murder on the 23rd of March 1801, and his son Aleksandr Pavlovič Romanov, that with the title of Alexander I, sat on the throne until the 1st December 1825.

Our reprint in based on the original 19th century volumes, to be precise the volumes from 7 to 9 are dedicated to the reign of Paul I; this first part is distributed on 7 volumes, having a numbering from 1 to 7. From number 10 to 18 of the original volumes, the second part is dedicated to the Russian troops under Alexander I. These still being worked on and they will be soon ready, distributed on twenty volumes approximately. Our new edition, the first ever published in English, both on paper and digital format, boasts a large number of color plates, many of them unpublished and coloured by our team of expert artists and scholars of uniformology. Each volume is based on 50/70 plates, always accompanied by the original translated text which describes the uniforms, the organization and the armament of the Russian army of the period.

In this book we present the Russian Guards Garrison, Invalids, Marine équipage & Instructional corps of the Napoleonic wars. A unique work in its genre, a must have in any respecting collection!

Aleksandr Vasilevich Viskovatov born 22 April (4 May New Style) 1804, died 27 February (11 March) 1858 in St. Petersburg, Russian military historian. He graduated from the 1st Cadet Corps and served in the artillery, the hydrographic depot of the Naval Ministry, and then in the Department of Military Educational Institutions. He mainly studied historical artifacts and the histories of military units. Viskovatov's greatest work was the Historical Description of the Clothing and Arms of the Russian Army (Vols. 1-30, St. Petersburg, 1841-62; 2nd ed. Vols. 1-34, St. Petersburg - Novosibirsk - Leningrad, 1899-1948). This work is based on a great quantity of archival documents and contains four thousand colored illustrations.

Viskovatov was the author of Chronicles of the Russian Army (Books 1-20, St. Petersburg, 1834-42) and Chronicles of the Russian Imperial Army (Parts 1-7, St. Petersburg, 1852). He collected valuable material on the history of the Russian navy which went into A Short Overview of Russian Naval Campaigns and General Voyages to the End of the XVII Century (St. Petersburg, 1864; 2nd edition Moscow, 1946). Together with A.I. Mikhailovskii-Danilevskii he helped prepare and create the Military Gallery in the Winter Palace.

He wrote the historical military inscriptions for the walls of the Hall of St. George in the Great Palace of the Kremlin. (From the article in the Soviet Military Encyclopedia.)

CONTENTS

*

Preface pag. 5

*

Guards Garrison. pag. 7

Guards Invalids. pag. 9

Guards Equipage. pag. 9

Instructional corps. pag. 11

Notes pag. 14

*

PLATES pag. 17

RUSSIAN ARMY- GUARDS GARRISON

CHANGES IN THE UNIFORMS AND EQUIPMENT OF GUARDS GARRISON, INVALID,

MARINE EQUIPAGE & INSTRUCTIONAL CORPS FROM 1801 TO 1825.

XLVII . GUARDS GARRISON. *[Gvardeiskii garnizon.]*

In **1801** and **1802**, with the general change in Guards uniforms, there were no special directives for the **L.-Gds. Garrison Battalion**. It was only ordered to follow the example of the L.-Gds. Preobrazhenskii Regiment as it did during the preceding Reign, having white buttons; grenadier caps of regular army pattern with a red top, white tin front plate and band, and a red tassel in the center; silver embroidery on officers' coats, these being without aiguillettes (Illus. 2226 and 2227). Neither were officers authorized gorgets [147]. Based on this, the uniform clothing and weapons of the L.-Gds. Garrison Battalion underwent almost all the same changes as occurred in the L.-Gds. Preobrazhenskii Regiment.

19 October 1803 - Instead of just one, privates are ordered to have two **shoulder straps**.

19 October 1804 - Combatant lower ranks—instead of grenadier caps—are ordered to have a **cloth headdress** with a visor and thick hair plume (Illus. 2228). Beginning in this year, field and company-grade officers began to wear **hats** with a buttonhole loop of narrow silver galloon instead of embroidery, and with a high plume (Illus. 2229).

1 October 1806 - The sheepskin warm coats [*ovchinnnya fufaiki*] of lower ranks are discontinued.

10 March 1807 - Officers' spontoons are abolished. In this same year the **queues** of lower ranks were cut short, while in this regard officers were allowed to proceed according to their own wishes.

17 September 1807 - Officers are given silver **epaulettes** [*epolety*], the same color as their buttons (Illus. 2230). In this year they began to wear **boots** below the knee, without cut-outs in back, and cut off their **queues**, continuing to powder their hair only for grand parades and appearances at HIGHEST Court.

26 September and **19 December 1807** - Lower ranks were ordered to wear their **sword belts** over the shoulder (Illus. 2231).

23 December 1807 - Lower ranks are given new pattern summer and winter **pants**: the first with spats and the second with leather cuffs provided with seven brass buttons (Illus. 2231).

16 April 1808 - Lower ranks are given **shakos** [*kivera*] with a plate, cords of red and yellow wool, and a pyramidal plume (Illus. 2231). Officers, when in formation or on other duties, receive the same shakos with those distinctions that distinguishes them from lower ranks. In this same year, the previous embroidery on their coats was replaced by **buttonhole loops** (Illus. 2232).

14 July 1808 - The round **knapsacks** prescribed for use by lower ranks are exchanged for rectangular ones, and the manner of wearing it is defined, as is the method of carrying the greatcoat when that item is not being worn.

5 November 1808 - Company-grade officers, when the troops are wearing **knapsacks**, are ordered to also have them, in all ways of the same pattern as is established for lower ranks.

12 November 1808 - Field and company-grade officers, when not on duty, are allowed to wear dark-green cloth **pants** instead of white ones.

4 April 1809 - Non-commissioned officers are ordered to sew galloon not on the lower and side edges of the collar, but on the upper and side edges.

8 April 1809 - The lower bracket on the **musket** stock, for the sling, is to be moved higher up to the brass trigger guard. The button on the sling is to be located two fingers from the upper sling bracket. A buckle with prong is to be fixed to the middle of the ramrod's brass lower band or tube, and the upper side, i.e. the side painted red, of the sling is to be lacquered so that it would not stain the pouch crossbelt.

20 April 1809 - Supplementary instructions are issued for the directives of 14 July 1808 concerning **knapsacks** and **greatcoats**.

30 May 1809 - Non-commissioned officers with muskets and front pouches [*podsumki*] have the latter item replaced with **pouches** [*sumy*] of the same pattern as for privates. Consequently, these men as well as all personnel of non-commissioned officer rank, and also company drummers and fifers, are given **shoulder straps** on both shoulders (Illus. 2233).

29 August 1809 - Halberds are retained only for first sergeants [*feldfebeli*], while all other non-commissioned officers were given muskets identical to soldiers'.

1 September 1809 - Confirmation was given to a **table of uniform clothing** and other items for the battalion, based on which its uniforms remain as before.

6 December 1809 - Officers' **shakos** are given the same plumes as for lower ranks, and scales for the chinstrap instead of the small chain (Illus. 2234) In this same year officers were given **frock coats** and their canes and hair powder were abolished.

10 February 1810 - Chinscales are added to lower ranks' **shakos**, which at the same time are ordered to have white cords instead of multi-colored ones, except for non-commissioned officers with their multi-colored tassels and slides (Illus. 2235). Officers receive entirely silver cords, and for all combatant ranks in the battalion a new pattern shako plume is confirmed, narrower at the bottom than at the top (Illus. 2235 and 2236). Also, the plumes on officers' **hats** are shortened (Illus. 2236).

23 September 1811 - All ranks are ordered to have **forage caps** of the new pattern, dark green with a red band, plus a cockade for officers.

9 October 1811 - The **halberds** that had been retained by first sergeants are withdrawn, and they were given muskets and cartridge pouches.

3 November 1811 - Gloves are discontinued for non-commissioned officers, and in this same year their canes were withdrawn.

January 1812 - All combatant ranks were given: a **shako** lower than before, with a concave top; **collars** closed by small hooks; for lower ranks only sewn-on tape of yellow with orange stripes and a red light; integral **leggings** [*kragi*] reaching up to the knees, with nine buttons (Illus. 2237 and 2238).

In **1814** white tape was added around the **cockades** of officers' hats, which later became silver.

31 December 1815 - The L.-Gds. Garrison Battalion is ordered to have, instead of red **collars**, dark-green collars with red piping (Illus. 2239, 2240, and 2241) [148].

24 January 1816 - The **scabbards** for short swords [*tesaki*] and officers' swords [*shpagi*] are ordered to be black and lacquered.

13 May, 8 August, and **26 September 1817** - Instructions were issued regarding: the soldier's **marching uniform**, the dimensions of his **forage cap**, and the construction and wearing of **accouterments**.

8 December 1817 - Lower ranks are given spat-like projections [*kozyr'ki*] to the leather cuffs on **pants**.

23 August 1818 - The length and width of **shoulder straps** are defined.

4 April 1819 - The **spats** on the leggings are removed.

In **1820** there were changes in the uniforms of **musicians, fifers, and drummers**, consisting of their sewn-on chevrons beginning to be placed closer together, almost touching one another, and on the swallows' nests the tape was no longer perpendicular as before, but at a diagonal toward the lower edge. Also, all four sides of the collar began to be trimmed with this tape (Illus. 2242).

26 November 1823 - All the battalion's **musicians**, even though they might not hold non-commissioned officer ranks, are ordered to have: silver galloon on the coat; plumes on the shakos with non-commissioned officers' tops and non-commissioned officers' pompons. This does not apply to fifers and drummers who do not hold non-commissioned officer rank.

8

16 January 1824 - The following changes are ordered in the uniforms and accouterments of combatant lower ranks:

1) **Coattails**, which up to this time had one covering the other, are to be cut so that their inner edges came together, and sewn together where they touched (Illus. 22434).

2.) To the decorative end [*trinchik*] of the **shako cords**, which is to be level with the right shoulder, there is to be added a special loop of white cord attached to the button on the right shoulder strap, so that the shako cords stay in place when the soldier moves about (Illus. 2243).

3.) The **cartridge pouch** is to be worn so that when the soldier bent his elbow, the distance between it and a line with the top edge of the pouch is equal to 3 vershoks [5 1/4 inches].

4.) The **knapsack** chest strap is to be fitted so that it passes between the third and fourth buttons of the coat, as counted from the bottom (Illus. 2243).

5.) On the **musket sling**, opposite the cocking piece, there is to be a band of the same kind of leather as the sling, for stowing the flint cover [*ognivnyi chekhol*] when it needs to be removed (Illus. 2243).

In this same year officers as well as lower ranks began to wear a taller **shako** with wider cords (Illus. 2243 and 2244), but no specific instructions were officially issued for this.

29 March 1825 - For combatant lower ranks, for faultless service, there are established stripes [*nashivki*] to be sewn on the left sleeve: for 10 years service - one, for 15 years - two, for 20 years - three; one over the other, all of yellow tape [149].

XLVIII . GUARDS INVALIDS. *[Gvardeiskii invalid.]*

27 January 1809 - **Guards Invalid companies** are ordered to have: gray coat and pants, the first without any sewn-on lace, with red collar, shoulder straps, cuffs, and skirt turnbacks; boots reaching below the knee; and a forage cap of gray cloth with a red band and a gray and red tassel (Illus. 2245). Officers were uniformed as officers in the L.-Gds. Garrison Battalion but did not have buttonhole loops on their coats, nor shakos [150].

23 September 1811 - Lower ranks are given **forage caps** of a new pattern, identical to that introduced at this time throughout the Army, colored gray as before, with a red band on which was the company number in yellow (Illus. 2246) [151].

In **1812** the high open **collars** were replaced by lower ones closed with small hooks (Illus. 2246) [152].

31 December 1815 - Guards Invalid companies are given new **uniforms**, the same as received at this time by the L.-Gds. Garrison Battalion, but without piping on the collar, dark-green cuffs, and a shako without a plume. Lower ranks are given short swords [*tesaki*] on a white crossbelt (Illus. 2247 and 2248) [153]. Non-serving Guards Invalids, who would be disbanded in 1823, are ordered to have all items as for the preceding serving Invalids, but the coat and pants were gray (Illus. 2249) [154].

After **1815** the changes related above for the L.-Gds. Garrison Battalion were also applied to Guards Invalids, who in **1824** received taller **shakos** with wider cords than previously, with lower ranks also having tailcoats with the skirts sewn together (Illus. 2250 and 2251). Invalid personnel with the Guards troops in **Warsaw** were distinguished from other Guards Invalids by the **yellow** color of their cuff flaps and skirt turnbacks [155].

XLIX . GUARDS ÉQUIPAGE. *[Gvardeiskii Ekipazh.]*

23 February 1810 - A table of uniforms and other items for the **Guards Équipage** is confirmed, based on which the following are authorized:

For Privates (youths and sailors) [*Ryadovye (mladshie yungi i matrosy)*]: double-breasted jacket [*kurtka*] of dark-green cloth, with white cloth piping on the collar, cuffs, and cuff flaps; with Guards checkered tape sewn on the collar and cuff flaps; red shoulder straps and brass buttons; single-breasted (under the jacket) vest [*zhilet*] of dark-green cloth, without sleeves, with covered buttons; winter pants of dark-green cloth, and summer ones of Flemish linen; boots and neckcloth, of the same patterns as for other Infantry; round black hat with a Guards pattern plate to which is added only two crossed anchors (Illus. 2252 and 2253); greatcoat, of normal infantry pattern, of gray cloth, with collar and shoulder straps of the same colors as on the jacket, with brass buttons. In summertime, when not on duty they are to wear a jacket and pants of striped ticking (white with dark blue), patterned after the cloth items except that the first has covered buttons and no shoulder straps, cuffs, or cuff flaps (Illus. 2254). Under the summer jacket is worn a white vest of ticking with one row of covered buttons [156].

Non-commissioned officers (quartermasters, boatswain mates, and boatswains [*Unter-ofitsery (kvartirmeistery, botsman-maty i botsmany)*]) are distinguished by gold galloon on the collar and cuffs on the cloth jacket, and have gloves and a cane (Illus. 2255). Their summer clothing is not striped but white (Illus. 2256) [157].

Of noncombatant ranks, the assistant storekeeper and cooks [*unter-bataler i povara*] are uniformed as privates, while the storekeeper, medical orderly, clerk, and steersman assistants [*bataler, fel'dsher, klerk i shkiperskie pomoshchniki*] as non-commissioned officers [158].

Company-grade officers (Midshipmen and Lieutenants [*Michmany i Leitenanty*]) wear a dark-green double-breasted tail-coat with the same buttons as throughout the Guards Infantry, with gold embroidery on the collar and cuff flaps depicting an anchor fouled with rope and cable; gold edging on the collar, cuffs, and cuff flaps; gold epaulettes as for all Guards company-grade officers, with red cloth backing (Illus. 2257 and 2258). Dark-green cloth pants are prescribed for winter dress, and in summer—white linen. In both seasons they wear an infantry pattern three-cornered hat without a plume, and an officer's sword [*shpaga*] with a silver sword knot (Illus. 2257). Field-grade officers (Captain-Lieutenant and 1st or 2nd Rank Captain [*Kapitan-Leitenant i Kapitan 2-go ili 1-go ranga*]) are distinguished only by fringe on the epaulettes (Illus. 2259). When not on duty all officers wear a double-breasted dark-green undress coat [*vitse-mundir*] with embroidered gold buttonhole loops on the collar and cuff flaps, and instead of a sword—a dagger [*kortik*] with a white bone handle and gilt fittings. Officers' greatcoats are the same as in the Army, with a dark-green cloth collar [159].

Cannoneers of the Guards Équipage Artillery Command [*Artilleriiskoi komandy Gvardeiskago Ekipazha kanoniry*] are uniformed like sailors, but instead of dark-green collars and cuffs they have black, and on their hats are two crossed cannons. Bombardiers [*bombardiry*] are distinguished by gold galloon on the collar and wore gloves. They have a cane and a short sword [*tesak*] in a black lacquered scabbard on a likewise black lacquered crossbelt that is two vershoks [3-1/2 inches] wide (Illus. 2261). The metalsmith [*slesar'*] in the command is uniformed the same as cannoneers, and the commissioned officers (Sub-Lieutenant and Lieutenant [*Unter-Leitenant i Leitenant*]) differ from the Équipage officers only in the black color of the collar and cuffs (Illus. 2262) [160].

In **1811** non-commissioned officers' **gloves** and **canes** were withdrawn, as were all lower ranks' winter and summer vests and **summer clothing** except for the white pants prescribed for wear with the cloth jackets. In place of round hats, the Équipage's privates were given the infantry **shakos** of that time, with the same plate as the hat, white cords, and a dark-green pompon. They also received infantry **muskets** and jäger pouches with a brass anchor on the cover, along with attached bayonet scabbards (Illus. 2263). Non-commissioned officers of the Équipage received shakos, muskets, pouches, and infantry short swords with non-commissioned officers' sword knots (Illus. 2264). The **Artillery detachment** received shakos with red cords and pompon, and bombardiers and cannoneers were given short swords and pouches on crossbelts, on one of which were prickers (Illus. 2265) Along with these changes, the Équipage was authorized **drummers, fifers, and musicians**, uniformed as the other combatant lower ranks, with the distinctions established for all Guards Infantry, the drum hoops and drumsticks being black (Illus. 2266 and 2267). **Officers** in formation or on parade were ordered to also be in shakos, and instead of swords, they were to always have sabers, with a gilded hilt and a scabbard of black lacquered leather. Hooks and chape were gilded. These sabers were worn on a crossbelt of black lacquered leather over the right shoulder, over the coat (Illus. 2268) [161].

In **1812** the **shakos** and **collars** began to be lower than before, the first with a concave top and the second without a diagonal opening in front, being closed with small hooks and having, for lower ranks, the same sewn-on **tape** as the rest of the Guards (Illus. 2269, 2270, 2271, and 2272) [162].

1817 - In regard to the shape of the **shako** and construction of **accouterments**, the Guards Équipage was guided by the same directives as set forth for the rest of the Guards on 26 September of that year, described in detail above for Grenadier regiments (Illus. 2273, 2274, 2275, and 2276) [163].

In **1820** the **tape** on the coats of drummers, fifers, and musicians began to be sewn on more closely together, and around the entire collar (Illus. 2277) [164].

In **1824** the **shako** began to become taller and the shako cords wider, the latter having a loop to attach to the button on the right shoulder strap and epaulette, as related above regarding shakos in the Army and Guards (Illus. 2278). Along with this, the **knapsack** chest strap was to be fitted between the fourth and fifth buttons of the coat instead of the second and third as was done before, counting from the collar [165].

29 March 1825 - For combatant lower ranks, for faultless service, there are established **stripes** [*nashivki*] to be sewn on the left sleeve, of yellow tape of the same appearance and according to the same rules as described above for the Army and Guards [166].

In addition to the uniform clothing items described here for the Guards Équipage, those field and company-grade officers who were prescribed to be mounted when in formation were given dark-green cloth **shabracks** and **pistol carriers**, with two rows of gold galloon and the usual pattern of Guards star in silver (Illus. 2279) [167].

L . INSTRUCTIONAL GRENADIER BATTALIONS and the INSTRUCTIONAL CARABINIER REGIMENT. *[Uchebnye grenaderskie bataliony i Uchebnyi Karabinernyi polk.]*

20 June 1808 - All uniform clothing, accouterments, and weapons for the **Instructional Grenadier Battalion** are prescribed to be the same as used at this time in Army Grenadier regiments, except that the shoulder straps were trimmed with two rows of woolen tape, colored red with yellow stripes along the sides and—between the stripes—yellow circles [*kruzhki*] (Illus. 2280, 2281, and 2282). The field on officers' epaulettes was not cloth, as in Grenadier regiments, but gold, in the manner of the Guards (Illus. 2283) [168]. Subsequent HIGHEST orders and regulations confirmed by HIGHEST Authority for Grenadier regiments, described above in full detail, were also extended to Instructional Grenadier battalions, viz.: **20 November 1808** - on having pants with leather cuffs only for combatant lower ranks; **5 November 1808** - on officers having knapsacks of the same pattern as lower ranks; **12 November** - on allowing officers to wear dark-green pants when not on duty; **November of 1808** - on changing the pattern for officers' gorgets; **11 February 1808** - on the changes in uniforms for noncombatant ranks; **4 April 1809** - on sewing non-commissioned officers' galloon not along the lower and side edges of the collar, but along the upper and side edges; **8 April 1809** - on the new manner of fitting the sling to the musket; **20 April 1809** - on the manner of carrying the greatcoat with the knapsack, and providing the knapsack with a strap across the chest; **30 May 1809** - on replacing front pouches, for non-commissioned officers with muskets, with pouches worn at the back; and **8 June 1809** - on privates having all-white shako cords, and non-commissioned officers— white with a mix of black and orange [169].

28 June 1809 - The newly established **second Instructional Grenadier Battalion** is prescribed all the same uniform clothing, accouterments, and weapons as the battalion formed in 1808 [170]. *(Note: on 15 August 1809 this battalion was ordered to be named the 2nd Instructional Grenadier Battalion, and the previous battalion—the 1st.)* Subsequent HIGHEST orders and regulations confirmed by HIGHEST Authority for Grenadier regiments, described above in full detail, were also extended to these two battalions, viz.: **29 August 1809** - on only sergeants having halberds, with other non-commissioned officers having muskets; **23 February 1809** - on the pompons in the 1st Battalion being white with a green center and in the 2nd—green with a white center; **6 December 1809** - on officers to wear shakos when in formation (Illus. 2284); **24 September 1810** - on making knapsack straps with stitching at the edges and with a curve at the shoulders; **17 January 1811** - on white shako cords for non-commissioned officers and musicians, with a mix of black and orange only in the tassels and slides [*gaiki*], and all-silver cords for officers; **29 January 1811** - on red cuffs for officers' frock coats, instead of dark green; **4 February 1811** - on new shako plumes, wider at the top and narrower at the bottom (Illus. 2285 and 2286); **22 February 1811** - on pompons, red in the 1st Battalion's Grenadier company, red with green below in the 2nd Battalion's Grenadier company, white with a green center in the 1st Battalion's Fusilier companies, and green with a white center in the 2nd Battalion's Fusilier companies, and on this same date—on red acorns, loops, and bands for sword knots in the 1st Battalion's Grenadier platoon; yellow acorns, loops and bands in the Marksmen platoon; white acorns, loops, and bands in the 1st Fusilier Company; sky-blue acorns, loops, and bands in the 2nd; orange acorns, loops, and bands in the 3rd; red acorns and green loops, and bands in the 2nd Battalion's Grenadier platoon; yellow acorns and green loops, and bands in the 2nd Battalion's Marksmen platoon; green acorns and white loops and bands in the 1st Fusilier Company; white acorns and sky-blue loops and bands in the 2nd; and white acorns and orange loops and bands in the 3rd [171].

16 July 1811 - The newly established **3rd Instructional Grenadier Battalion** is prescribed all the same uniform clothing, accouterments, and arms as the first two battalions [172]. Subsequent HIGHEST orders and regulations confirmed by

HIGHEST Authority for Grenadier regiments, described above in full detail, were also extended to all three Instructional-al Grenadier battalions, viz.: **23 September 1811** - on a new pattern forage cap, dark green with a red band and different piping for each company; **9 October 1811** - on sergeants exchanging their halberds for muskets; **3 November 1811** - on gloves being withdrawn from non-commissioned officers, and in this same year?on their canes being withdrawn and the plumes of officers' hats being shortened; **17 December 1811** - on noncombatant lower ranks being prescribed new uniforms of gray cloth with red piping; in **1812** - on having shakos lower than before, with a concave top; collars closed with small hooks and without a diagonal front opening; and leggings to the knees (Illus. 2287 and 2288); **10 February 1812** - on noncombatant lower ranks having the same pattern of shoulder straps as combatants; in **1814** - on officers wearing riding trousers without leather reinforcements or brass buttons, with wide red stripes and piping, and on the addition of white tape to the cockades on officers' hats, later changed to silver; and **24 January 1816** - on having the scabbards for short swords and bayonets of black polished leather, and for officers' swords—of black lacquered leather [173].

16 March 1816 - The **Instructional Carabinier Regiment**, formed from the Instructional Grenadier battalions, was ordered to have all the same uniform clothing, accouterments, and arms as Carabinier regiments in the Grenadier Corps, except that shoulder straps were to be trimmed with yellow tape [*bason*] with red longitudinal stripes, and officers' epaulettes were to have a gold field with no number. The shako was to have the plate established on **16 April 1817** for Grenadier and Carabinier regiments (Illus. 2289, 2290, 2291, and 2292), and officers' epaulettes were gold, without any cloth field (Illus. 2293 and 2294) [174]. Subsequent HIGHEST orders and regulations confirmed by HIGHEST Authority for Carabinier regiments, described above in full detail, were also extended to all the Instructional Carabinier Regiment, viz.: **13 May 1817** - on covers or cases for shakos, plumes, pouches, and the coat; **8 August 1817** - on the dimensions of the forage cap; **26 September 1817** - on patterns for accouterments and the manner of wearing them; **8 December 1817** - on spat-like projections [*kozyr'ki*]on the leather cuffs of pants; **23 August 1818** - on the size of crossbelts over the shoulder and on wings for the coats of drummers, fifers, and musicians being of red cloth instead of yellow, and sewn-on tape have a white stripe down the center (Illus. 2295); **4 April 1819** - on the removal of spats from pants cuffs; **10 April 1819** - on uniforming hornists the same as drummers; **20 September 1820** - on new pattern gorgents for officers (Illus. 2296), and in the same year—on sewn-on tape for the coats of drummers, hornists, fifers, and musicians being spaced more closely than before (Illus. 2297); **26 November 1823** - on all musicians to have non-commissioned officer galloon, pompons, sword knots, and plumes; and **24 January 1824** - on sewing coattails together, adding a loop to the decorative end of the shako cords, wearing the knapsack chest strap between the fourth and fifth buttons, counting from the collar, and on adding a band to the musket sling for the firing cover. Since **1824** the Instructional Carabinier Regiment, after the example of other regiments, began to wear taller shakos and wider shako cords than before (Illus. 2298 and 2299) [175].

LI. INSTRUCTIONAL CAVALRY SQUADRON. *[Uchebnyi Kavaleriiskii eskadron.]*

22 April 1809 - The **Instructional Cavalry Squadron** is prescribed all the same uniform clothing, accouterments, and arms and laid down in this year for Army Dragoon regiments, except with shoulder straps of the pattern used in Instructional Grenadier battalions (red with yellow tracery). Collar, cuffs, coattail lining and turnbacks, and saddlecloth trim were red. Buttons were yellow (Illus. 2300, 2301, and 2302 [176]. Subsequent HIGHEST orders and regulations confirmed by HIGHEST Authority for Army Dragoon regiments, described above in detail, were also extended to all the Instructional Cavalry Squadron, viz.: **16 June 1810** - on making musketoons according to a new pattern and henceforth calling them dragoon muskets; **16 September 1811** - on the removal of buckles, prongs, and end pieces from cartridge-pouch belts, as well as belt hooks and the rings on the pouch itself; **23 September 1811** - on the introduction of new pattern forage caps of dark-green cloth with a red band; **11 December 1811** - on new pattern uniform clothing for noncombatant lower ranks, being gray with red piping; in **1812** - on having collars lower than before, without the diagonally open front, and closed by small hooks (Illus. 2303), and on withdrawing muskets; **20 May** and **19 August 1814** - on having riding trousers without buttons, with wide stripes and piping in the color of the collar; in **1817** - on officers wearing pouches when in formation, on lower ranks' helmets being replaced by shakos with a grenadier plate, double-breasted coats being replaced by single-breasted, epaulettes replacing shoulder straps, dark-green chakchiry pants replacing white pants, with wide red stripes and piping, and the saber replacing the broadsword (Illus. 2304 and 2305); on trumpeters having wings the same color as the collar (Illus. 2306); **16 February 1820** - on the pattern for a shako cover; **20 February 1820** - on the removal of shako plumes; **7 August 1820** - on allowing officers to wear moustaches, and in the same year—on the tape on trumpeters' coats being sewn on more closely together (Illus. 2307). Since **1824**, taller shakos began to be worn in the Instructional Cavalry Squadron, and shako cords became wider and provided with a loop for attachment to the button of the right epaulette (Illus. 2308) [177].

LII . INSTRUCTIONAL ARTILLERY BRIGADE. *[Uchebnyi Artilleriiskaya brigada.]*

(Note: Before 1820 the companies that made up this brigade were part of the Guards Foot Artillery and had the same uniform, which can be seen from examination of HIGHEST Confirmed equipment tables for them.)

28 May 1820 - All uniform clothing, accouterments, and weapons for the **Instructional Artillery Brigade** are ordered to be the same as used in this year in Grenadier Artillery brigades, except that the shoulder straps of lower ranks are trimmed with tape, yellow with thin red stripes, and officers have epaulettes with a gold field instead of cloth, and no number, as in the Instructional Carabinier Regiment (Illus. 2309 and 2310)[178]. Subsequent orders in **1824** on sewing coattails together, adding a loop to the decorative right end of the shako cords, fitting the knapsack chest strap so that it passed between the fourth and fifth coat buttons as counted from the collar, and having taller shakos and wider shako cords (Illus. 2311 and 2312), were all applied to the Instructional Artillery Brigade [179].

LIII . INSTRUCTIONAL SAPPER BATTALION. *[Uchebnyi Sapernyi batalion.]*

21 May 1820 - The **Instructional Sapper Battalion** is ordered to have all uniform clothing, accouterments, and weapons the same as it had before being renamed from the 2nd Sapper Battalion, except that lower ranks' shoulder straps were to be as in the Instructional Carabinier Regiment and Instructional Artillery Brigade, and officers' epaulettes were to have a silver field instead of cloth, and without a number (Illus. 2313, 2314, and 2315) [180]. Subsequent HIGHEST orders of **26 November 1823** - on all musicians' coats to have non-commissioned officers' galloon and their shakos to have non-commissioned officers' pompons—and **16 January 1824** - on sewing coattails together, adding a loop to the decorative right end of the shako cords, fitting the knapsack chest strap so that it passed between the fourth and fifth coat buttons as counted from the collar, were all applied to the Instructional Sapper Battalion, which in 1824 began to wear taller shakos with wider shakos cords than before (Illus. 2316) [181].

▲ *The battle fought versus the Ney corps the 6 November 1812*

13

NOTES

(147) From the files of the same Department.

(148) PSZ Vol. XLIV, pg. 109, No. 26,058, and contemporary drawings and uniforms.

(149) Ibid., Vol. XL, pg. 188, No. 30,309.

(150) HIGHEST confirmed table of uniforms items for the Guards Invalid Company, 27 January 1809; from the files of the War Ministry's Commissariat Department, and information from contemporaries.

(151) From the same files and statements by contemporaries.

(152) Ditto.

(153) PSZ Vol. XLIV, pg. 109, No.26,058, and contemporary drawings and uniforms.

(154) Ditto.

(156) HIGHEST confirmed table for the Guards Équipage, 23 February 1819, and information from contemporaries.

(157) Ditto.

(158) Ditto.

(159) Historical description of the Guards Équipage, compiled by this équipage in 1820, and statements from persons who served in the unit from the time of its formation.

(160) HIGHEST confirmed table for the Guards Équipage, 23 February 1810, and information from contemporaries.

(161) *Historical Journal*, compiled in 1820 at the Guards Équipage, and statements from contemporaries.

(162) Statements from contemporaries.

(163) Statements from contemporaries and contemporary drawings.

(164) Ditto.

(165) Statements from contemporaries and contemporary drawings and shakos.

(166) See above, in all the notes for Army and Guards Infantry and Cavalry.

(167) Statements from contemporaries; contemporary drawings, and shabracks and pistol carriers still on hand at the present time.

(168) HIGHEST confirmed table of uniforms, accouterments, and weapons for the 3rd Instructional Grenadier Battalion, 20 July 1808, and from the files of the War Ministry's Commissariat Department.

(169) From the files of the War Ministry's Commissariat Department.

(170) Ditto.

(171) Ditto.

(172) HIGHEST confirmed table of uniforms, accouterments, and weapons for the Instructional Grenadier Battalion, 16 July 1811.

(173) From the files of the War Ministry's Commissariat Department.

(174) PSZ Vol. XXXIII, No. 26,198, pg. 558, and from the files of the War Ministry's Commissariat Department.

(175) From the files of the War Ministry's Commissariat Department, and contemporary drawings.

(176) HIGHEST Confirmed table of accouterments and weapons for the Instructional Cavalry Squadron, 22 August 1809, and from the files of the War Ministry's Commissariat Department.

(177) From the files of the War Ministry's Commissariat Department.

(178) HIGHEST Confirmed table of uniforms, accouterments, and other items for the two Battery and one Light companies of the Instructional Artillery Brigade, 28 May 1820; from the files of the War Ministry's Commissariat Department, and contemporary drawings.

(179) From the files of the War Ministry's Commissariat Department, and contemporary drawings.

(180) PSZ Vol. XXXVIII, No. 29,009, pg. 60 § 13.

(181) From the files of the War Ministry's Commissariat Department, and contemporary drawings.

▲ *The battle of Borodino of the 26 August 1812*

РИСУНКИ
ОДЕЖДЫ и ВООРУЖЕНІЯ
РОССІЙСКИХЪ
ВОЙСКЪ
1801-1825.

PLATES LIST OF ILLUSTRATIONS

2270. Company-Grade Officer. Guards Équipage, 1812-1816.

2271. Officer's Embroidery for the Guards Équipage, since 1812.

2272. Non-Commissioned Officer and Bombardier. Artillery Command of the Guards Équipage, 1812-1816.

2273. Sailors. Guards Équipage, 1817-1823.

2274. Non-Commissioned Officer and Drummer. Guards Équipage, 1817-1819.

2275. Company-Grade Officers. Guards Équipage, 1817-1823.

2276. Company-Grade Officer and Cannoneer. Artillery Command of the Guards Équipage, 1817-1823.

2277. Fifer. Guards Équipage, 1820-1823.

2278. Company-Grade Officer and Non-Commissioned Officer. Guards Équipage, 1824-1825.

2279. Field-Grade Officer. Guards Équipage, 1824-1825.

2280. Grenadiers. Instructional Grenadier Battalions, 1808-1809.

2281. Grenadier and Non-Commissioned Officer. Instructional Grenadier Battalions, 1808-1809.

2282. Drummer. Instructional Grenadier Battalions, 1808-1810.

2283. Company-Grade Officer. Instructional Grenadier Battalions, 1808-1810.

2284. Company-Grade Officer. Instructional Grenadier Battalions, 1809.

2285. Private. Instructional Grenadier Battalions, 1811.

2286. Non-Commissioned Officer. Instructional Grenadier Battalions, 1811.

2287. Private and Non-Commissioned Officer. Instructional Grenadier Battalions, 1812-1816.

2288. Drummer and Company-Grade Officer. Instructional Grenadier Battalions, 1812-1816.

2289. Private and Non-Commissioned Officer. Instructional Carabinier Regiment, 1816-1823.

2290. Private and Non-Commissioned Officer. Instructional Carabinier Regiment, 1816-1823.

2291. Jäger Drummer. Instructional Carabinier Regiment, 1816-1823.

2292. Musician. Instructional Carabinier Regiment, 1816-1818.

2293. Company-Grade Officers. Instructional Carabinier Regiment, 1816-1823.

2294. Field-Grade Officer. Instructional Carabinier Regiment, 1816-1820.

2295. Drummer and Fifer. Instructional Carabinier Regiment, 1818-1819.

2296. Field-Grade Officer. Instructional Carabinier Regiment, 1820-1823.

2297. Musician. Instructional Carabinier Regiment, 1820-1823.

2298. Jäger and Carabinier. Instructional Carabinier Regiment, 1824-1825.

2299. Field-Grade Officer. Instructional Carabinier Regiment, 1824-1825.

2300. Private. Instructional Cavalry Squadron, 1809-1811.

2301. Non-Commissioned Officer and Trumpeter. Instructional Cavalry Squadron, 1809-1811.

2302. Company-Grade Officer. Instructional Cavalry Squadron, 1809-1811.

2303. Non-Commissioned Officer and Company-Grade Officer. Instructional Cavalry Squadron, 1812-1816.

2304. Private and Non-Commissioned Officer. Instructional Cavalry Squadron, 1817-1820.

2305. Company-Grade Officers. Instructional Cavalry Squadron, 1817-1823.

2306. Trumpeter. Instructional Cavalry Squadron, 1817-1819.

2307. Trumpeter. Instructional Cavalry Squadron, 1820-1823.

2308. Non-Commissioned Officer and Company-Grade Officer. Instructional Cavalry Squadron, 1824-1825.

2309. Cannoneer and Non-Commissioned Officer [Feierverker]. Instructional Artillery Brigade, 1820-1823.

2310. Company-Grade Officer and Drummer. Instructional Artillery Brigade, 1820-1823.

2311. Non-Commissioned Officer [Feierverker] and Bombardier. Instructional Artillery Brigade, 1824-1825.

2312. Company-Grade Officer. Instructional Artillery Brigade, 1824-1825.

2313. Private and Non-Commissioned Officer. Instructional Sapper Battalion, 1822-1823.

2314. Drummer. Instructional Sapper Battalion, 1822-1823.

2315. Field-Grade Officer. Instructional Sapper Battalion, 1822-1823.

2316. Private and Company-Grade Officer. Instructional Sapper Battalion, 1824-1825.

Private and Non-Commissioned Officer. L.-Gds. Garrison Battalion, 1801-1804.

2227

Company-Grade Officer. L.-Gds. Garrison Battalion, 1801-1804

2228

Private. L.-Gds. Garrison Battalion, 1804-1807.

2229

Field-Grade Officer. L.-Gds. Garrison Battalion, 1804-1807.

2230

Company-Grade Officer. L.-Gds. Garrison Battalion, 1807-1808.

2231

Non-Commissioned Officer and Musician. L.-Gds. Garrison Battalion, 1808-1809.

Company-Grade Officer. L.-Gds. Garrison Battalion, 1808-1809.

2233

Non-Commissioned Officer. L.-Gds. Garrison Battalion, 1809

2234

Company-Grade Officer. L.-Gds. Garrison Battalion, 1809-1811.

2235

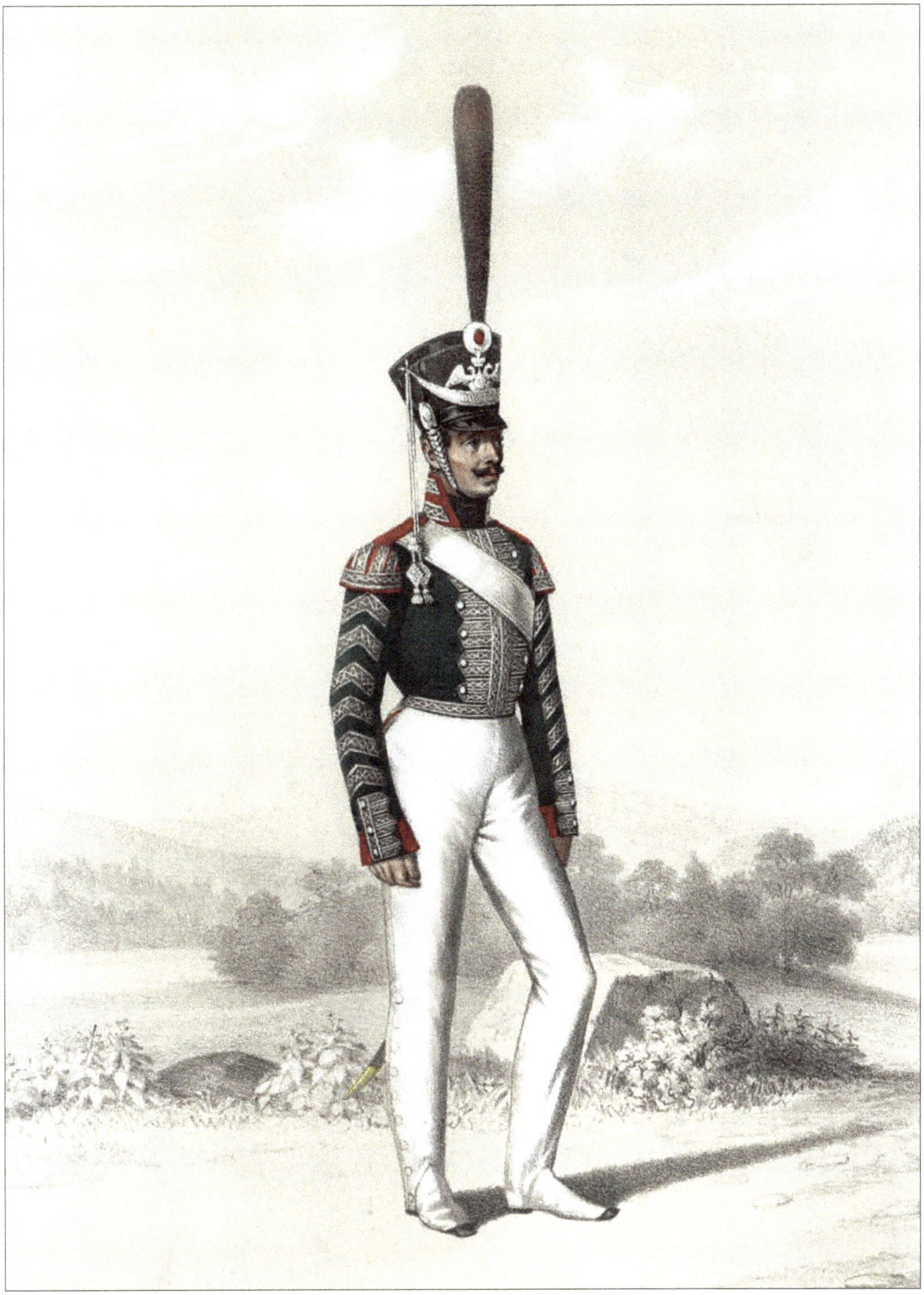

Drummer. L.-Gds. Garrison Battalion, 1810-1812.

2236

Company-Grade Officer and Field-Grade Officer. L.-Gds. Garrison Battalion, 1811-1812.

30

2237

Non-Commissioned Officer. L.-Gds. Garrison Battalion, 1812-1815.

31

2238

Company-Grade Officer. L.-Gds. Garrison Battalion, 1812-1815.

2239

Private. L.-Gds. Garrison Battalion, 1816-1824.

33

2240

Drummer. L.-Gds. Garrison Battalion, 1816-1819.

34

2241

Company-Grade Officer. L.-Gds. Garrison Battalion, 1816-1824.

2242

Drummer. L.-Gds. Garrison Battalion, 1820-1824.

36

Company-Grade Officer and Non-Commissioned Officer. L.-Gds. Garrison Battalion, 1824-1825.

Private. Guards Invalid Companies, 1809-1811.

2246

Non-Commissioned Officer. Guards Invalid Companies, 1812-1815.

Private. Guards Invalid Companies, 1816-1824.

2248

Company-Grade Officer. Guards Invalid Companies, 1816-1824.

41

Guards Non-Serving Invalid. 1816-1823.

Non-Commissioned Officer. Guards Invalid Companies, 1824-1825.

Company-Grade Officer and Private. Guards Invalid Companies Nos. 14-15, 1819-1825.

Sailors. Guards Équipage, 1810. (In winter and summer formation uniform.)

Shako plate for the Guards Équipage, 1810-1825. - Officer's Embroidery for the Guards Équipage, since 1812.

2254

Sailor. Guards Équipage, 1810. (In summer and everyday uniform.)

Non-Commissioned Officer. Guards Équipage, 1810. (In summer formation uniform.)

Non-Commissioned Officer. Guards Équipage, 1810. (In summer non-formation uniform.)

Company-Grade Officer and Field-Grade Officer. Guards Équipage, 1810. (In winter and summer uniform.)

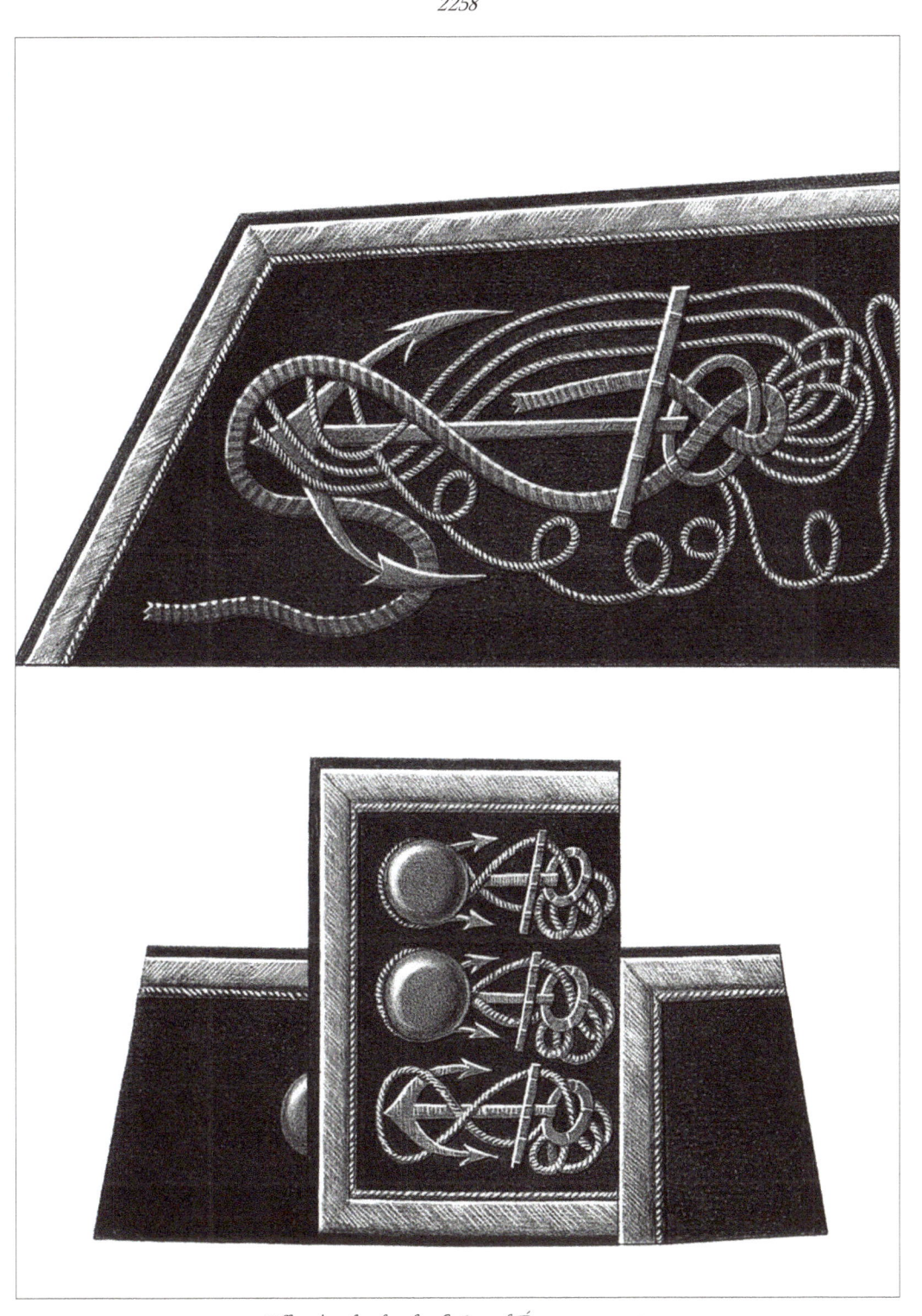

Officers' embroidery for the Guards Équipage, 1810-1811.

2259

Field-Grade Officer. Guards Équipage, 1810-1811. (In undress coat.)

Cannoneer and Bombardier. Artillery Command of the Guards Équipage, 1810. (In winter uniform.)

Non-Commissioned Officer. Artillery Command of the Guards Équipage, 1810. (In winter uniform.)

2262

Company-Grade Officers. Artillery Command of the Guards Équipage, 1810. (In summer uniform and undress coat.)

Sailors. Guards Équipage, 1811.

2264

Non-Commissioned Officer. Guards Équipage, 1811.

2265

Bombardier and Non-Commissioned Officer. Artillery Command of the Guards Équipage, 1811.

2266

Drummers. Guards Équipage and its Artillery Command, 1811.

59

Fifer and Musician. Guards Équipage, 1811.

Company-Grade Officers. Guards Équipage and its Artillery Command, 1811.

2269

Sailor and Non-Commissioned Officer. Guards Équipage, 1812-1816.

2270

Company-Grade Officer. Guards Équipage, 1812-1816.

63

2272

Non-Commissioned Officer and Bombardier. Artillery Command of the Guards Équipage, 1812-1816.

64

Sailors. Guards Équipage, 1817-1823.

2274

Non-Commissioned Officer and Drummer. Guards Équipage, 1817-1819.

2275

Company-Grade Officers. Guards Équipage, 1817-1823.

67

Company-Grade Officer and Cannoneer. Artillery Command of the Guards Équipage, 1817-1823.

2277

Fifer. Guards Équipage, 1820-1823.

2278

Company-Grade Officer and Non-Commissioned Officer. Guards Équipage, 1824-1825.

70

2279

Field-Grade Officer. Guards Équipage, 1824-1825.

2280

Grenadiers. Instructional Grenadier Battalions, 1808-1809.

2281

Grenadier and Non-Commissioned Officer. Instructional Grenadier Battalions, 1808-1809.

Drummer. Instructional Grenadier Battalions, 1808-1810.

2283

Company-Grade Officer. Instructional Grenadier Battalions, 1808-1810.

2284

Company-Grade Officer. Instructional Grenadier Battalions, 1809.

2285

Private. Instructional Grenadier Battalions, 1811.

2286

Non-Commissioned Officer. Instructional Grenadier Battalions, 1811.

2287

Private and Non-Commissioned Officer. Instructional Grenadier Battalions, 1812-1816.

Drummer and Company-Grade Officer. Instructional Grenadier Battalions, 1812-1816.

2289

Private and Non-Commissioned Officer. Instructional Carabinier Regiment, 1816-1823.

2290

Private and Non-Commissioned Officer. Instructional Carabinier Regiment, 1816-1823.

82

2291

Jäger Drummer. Instructional Carabinier Regiment, 1816-1823.

83

Musician. Instructional Carabinier Regiment, 1816-1818.

2293

Company-Grade Officers. Instructional Carabinier Regiment, 1816-1823.

2294

Field-Grade Officer. Instructional Carabinier Regiment, 1816-1820.

86

2295

Drummer and Fifer. Instructional Carabinier Regiment, 1818-1819.

Field-Grade Officer. Instructional Carabinier Regiment, 1820-1823.

2297

Musician. Instructional Carabinier Regiment, 1820-1823.

89

Jäger and Carabinier. Instructional Carabinier Regiment, 1824-1825

2299

Field-Grade Officer. Instructional Carabinier Regiment, 1824-1825.

2300

Private. Instructional Cavalry Squadron, 1809-1811.

Non-Commissioned Officer and Trumpeter. Instructional Cavalry Squadron, 1809-1811.

2302

Company-Grade Officer. Instructional Cavalry Squadron, 1809-1811.

94

2303

Non-Commissioned Officer and Company-Grade Officer. Instructional Cavalry Squadron, 1812-1816.

Private and Non-Commissioned Officer. Instructional Cavalry Squadron, 1817-1820.

2305

Company-Grade Officers. Instructional Cavalry Squadron, 1817-1823.

97

2306

Trumpeter. Instructional Cavalry Squadron, 1817-1819.

2307

Trumpeter. Instructional Cavalry Squadron, 1820-1823.

2308

Non-Commissioned Officer and Company-Grade Officer. Instructional Cavalry Squadron, 1824-1825.

100

2309

Cannoneer and Non-Commissioned Officer [Feierverker]. Instructional Artillery Brigade, 1820-1823.

Company-Grade Officer and Drummer. Instructional Artillery Brigade, 1820-1823.

Non-Commissioned Officer [Feierverker] and Bombardier. Instructional Artillery Brigade, 1824-1825.

2312

Company-Grade Officer. Instructional Artillery Brigade, 1824-1825.

104

Private and Non-Commissioned Officer. Instructional Sapper Battalion, 1822-1823.

2314

Drummer. Instructional Sapper Battalion, 1822-1823.

2315

Field-Grade Officer. Instructional Sapper Battalion, 1822-1823.

2316

Private and Company-Grade Officer. Instructional Sapper Battalion, 1824-1825.

SOLDIERS, WEAPONS & UNIFORMS ALREADY PUBLISHED
(SOME TITLES)

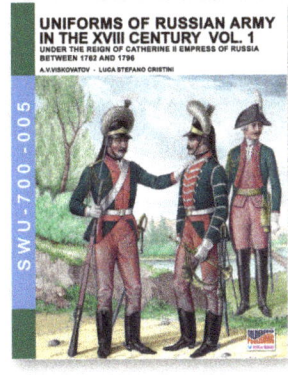

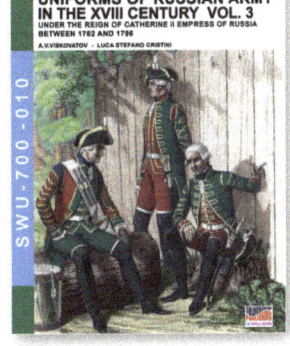

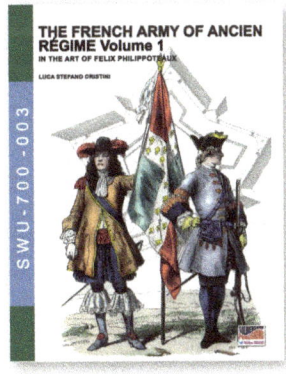

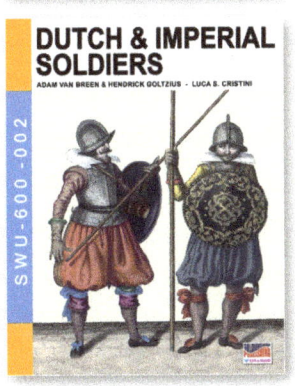
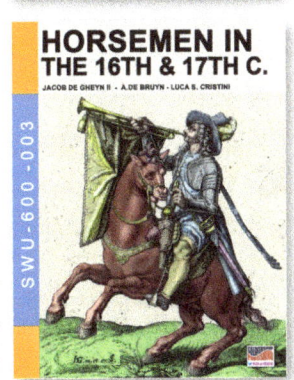

www.ingramcontent.com/pod-product-compliance
Lightning Source LLC
Chambersburg PA
CBHW041145120626
46547CB00020B/3121